RISKY JOBS

SEARCH AND RESCUE WORKER

JENNA TOLLI

PowerKiDS press

Published in 2025 by The Rosen Publishing Group, Inc.
2544 Clinton Street, Buffalo, NY 14224

First Edition

Editor: Jenna Tolli
Book Design: Rachel Rising

Photo Credits: Cover, Ground Picture/Shutterstock.com; Cover, pp. 1, 3–24 Apostrophe/Shutterstock.com; Cover, pp. 1, 3–24 cobalt88/Shutterstock.com; Cover, pp. 1, 3–24 ReVelStockArt/Shutterstock.com; p. 5 Dolores M. Harvey/Shutterstock.com; p. 7 jasomtomo/Shutterstock.com; pp. 8, 9, 20 hxdbzxy/Shutterstock.com; p. 11 SpiritProd33/Shutterstock.com; p. 12 Nikola Spasenoski/Shutterstock.com; p. 13 Tara Lambourne/Shutterstock.com; p. 14 Archaeonavall/Shutterstock.com; p. 15 Aidan Lambe/Shutterstock.com; p. 16 EB Adventure Photography/Shutterstock.com; p. 17 Dario Ravetto Creative/Shutterstock.com; p. 18 Imageforge/Shutterstock.com; p. 19 Sundry Photography/Shutterstock.com; p. 21 VDB Photos/Shutterstock.com.

Library of Congress Cataloging-in-Publication Data

Names: Tolli, Jenna, author.
Title: Search and rescue worker / Jenna Tolli.
Description: [Buffalo] : PowerKids Press, [2025] | Series: Risky jobs | Includes bibliographical references and index.
Identifiers: LCCN 2024007328 (print) | LCCN 2024007329 (ebook) | ISBN 9781499446166 (library binding) | ISBN 9781499446159 (paperback) | ISBN 9781499446173 (ebook)
Subjects: LCSH: Search and rescue operations–Juvenile literature. | Rescue work–Juvenile literature. | Volunteer workers in search and rescue operations–Juvenile literature.
Classification: LCC TL553.8 .T65 2025 (print) | LCC TL553.8 (ebook) | DDC 363.34/81–dc23/eng/20240216
LC record available at https://lccn.loc.gov/2024007328
LC ebook record available at https://lccn.loc.gov/2024007329

Manufactured in the United States of America

Some of the images in this book illustrate individuals who are models. The depictions do not imply actual situations or events.
CPSIA Compliance Information: Batch #CSPK25. For Further Information contact Rosen Publishing at 1-800-237-9932.

CONTENTS

SEARCH AND RESCUE

Search and rescue workers help find missing people and get them to safety. When people get lost or hurt in a place that's hard to get to, search and rescue teams get called in to help. Search and rescue is also known as SAR.

People with different types of jobs complete search and rescue operations. Police departments, fire departments, park rangers, and the U.S. military all have search and rescue teams. There are SAR teams on the ground, in the water, and in the air. This work can be very dangerous, and people need special training to do it.

DANGER!

Some people have jobs in search and rescue work, but there are also many **volunteers**. Sometimes volunteers will keep looking for someone after official teams need to end their search.

SAR teams have special skill sets that can help during different types of search and rescue operations.

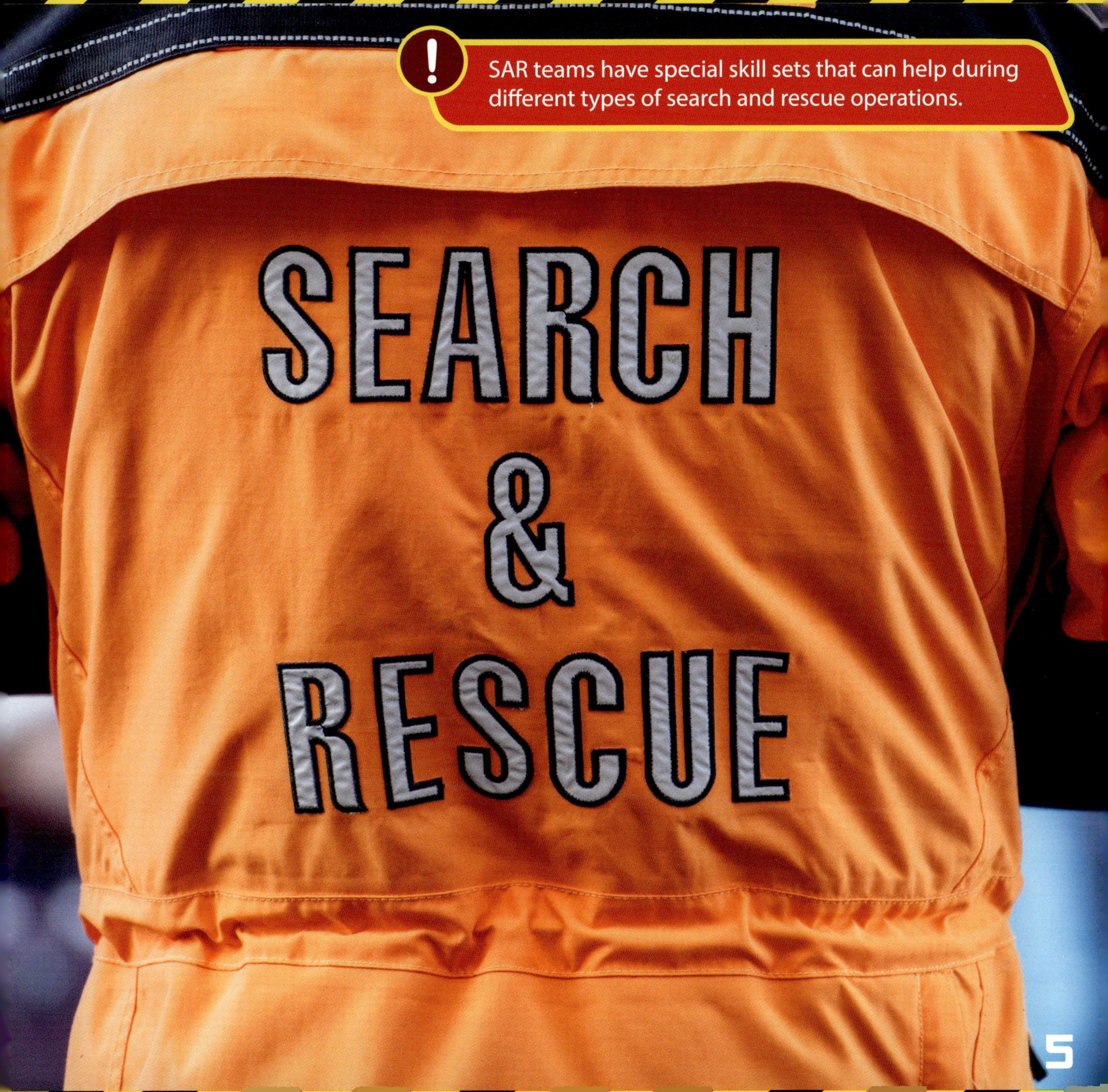

STARTING THE SEARCH

Finding the person who needs help is the first step of a SAR operation. Usually someone will call 911 to report a person as missing. This is when an **investigation** starts. SAR workers might search for the person on foot or use cars, snowmobiles, or horses. They might also search by boat, plane, or helicopter. Searches can take hours or even days.

After the person is found, they may need to be rescued. If they're trapped, the team will try to get them out and to safety. This can happen after hurricanes, earthquakes, or **avalanches**. They may also need **emergency** medical help.

DANGER!

In 2010, 33 people were trapped in an underground mine in Chile after an **accident**. The search took 17 days, and the rescue took 52 days. All the people were rescued.

Sometimes teams use search and rescue dogs. These teams are called K-9 units, or groups. Dogs use their strong sense of smell to find missing people.

MEDICAL HELP

Emergency medical technicians, also known as EMTs, treat people who need medical attention. They're usually the first ones on the scene to give first aid when someone is hurt. They can take people to hospitals for more help.

Some EMTs complete extra training to help with search and rescue work. They're called rescue EMTs. In addition to providing medical care, rescue EMTs have to know how to get people out of dangerous situations and how to safely move them if they are injured, or hurt. They can also give people medicine to help them with pain if they need it.

When people get hurt in emergencies like building **collapses** or car accidents, EMTs are trained to move them without causing more injuries.

POLICE SAR TEAMS

Police officers handle emergencies and solve crimes. They also do search and rescue work when someone is missing in their area. This could be when someone is reported as missing; if there is a **disaster**, like a building collapse; or if there is a crime, like a kidnapping. Police need to start working on a case very quickly.

Some police departments, especially ones in big cities, have their own SAR units. There are also volunteer groups that work with police departments to support, or help, search and rescue operations. Police often bring K-9 units on these searches.

DANGER!

SAR teams might also track someone's cell phone to try to find them. They can send a **signal** to their phone to find its location.

Police officers can use **drones** to help find missing people. They also use drones to see crime scenes from above.

FIRE RESCUE

Firefighters respond, or go, to fires to put them out. They find and rescue people who are trapped in burning buildings. It can be very hard for people to get out of a fire. They can pass out from breathing smoke or get trapped if part of the building collapses.

Rescuing people from burning buildings is very dangerous. Firefighters can get hurt or even killed on the job. Fire departments have special teams ready to rescue firefighters who have gone into buildings and become trapped or injured. These teams are called rapid intervention teams (RIT) or firefighter assist and search teams (FAST).

DANGER!

Firefighters don't just help people in fires. They are called to respond to many kinds of emergencies, including disaster events and car accidents, to help rescue people.

Fire SAR teams wear safety gear made for high temperatures. This includes special jackets and pants, gloves, helmets, and face masks.

AIR-SEA RESCUE

Sometimes there are emergencies in the water. A boat could sink, or a plane might need to make an emergency landing in the water. When people go missing in the water or need emergency help, the U.S. Coast Guard may be called. It may start a search and rescue operation using helicopters and boats.

The Coast Guard is part of the U.S. military. It protects the country's coasts and waters. The U.S. Coast Guard saves thousands of people each year, including over 5,000 in 2023. When the Coast Guard gets a **distress** call from someone at sea, it needs to act quickly.

This is a photo of a U.S. Coast Guard training operation. There are special training courses for search and rescue teams to practice their skills.

MOUNTAIN RESCUE

People can get hurt when they are hiking, climbing, skiing, or snowboarding. Sometimes people get lost because the weather makes it hard to see or move. SAR teams may be called in to find them and get them to safety. It is important to try and find someone within the first 24 hours.

Mountain SAR teams may include park rangers or state police, but these teams are often volunteers. SAR teams need to have experience in different outdoor activities. They are usually familiar with the area they support. Rescuers also need to know how to manage changing weather conditions.

DANGER!

For outdoor sports in **remote** locations, people should carry personal locator beacons. Beacons are small devices that send out signals of someone's location to help people find them in an emergency.

Mountain SAR teams may use special tools like ropes, harnesses, and ice screws to reach people in need. They will also need their own safety gear.

CIVIL AIR PATROL

The Civil Air Patrol flies over large areas for search and rescue operations. People in the patrol look for missing people and aircraft and provide emergency help during disasters. The Civil Air Patrol is an auxiliary of the U.S. Air Force. This means it offers and provides help and support.

The Civil Air Patrol is made up of over 60,000 volunteers across the United States. There are **civilian** pilots who fly the planes as well as flight crew members, ground crew members, engineers, and many others to support their operations. Each year, these people fly thousands of hours and rescue about 100 people.

The Civil Air Patrol has its own planes stationed across the country to use for its missions. A mission is a special job or task.

SAVING LIVES

To be a search and rescue worker, you need to be brave. People who work or volunteer on SAR teams enjoy helping their community and saving lives. There are many reasons that people choose to do SAR work. Some like to solve problems. Others like to be outdoors and use their skills to help in dangerous places and situations.

SAR teams put their lives in danger to help others. When they go into dangerous places, there's a chance that they'll get hurt, lost, or even killed. They sometimes risk their own lives to help people who need it the most.

Police departments, EMTs, firefighters, and rescue workers all work together to help with search and rescue operations.

GLOSSARY

accident: An unexpected and sometimes bad event.

avalanche: A large mass of ice, snow, or rock that slides down a mountain.

civilian: A person not on active duty in the military.

collapse: To break down or cave in.

disaster: Something that happens suddenly and causes much suffering and loss for many people.

distress: A condition of danger or desperate need.

drone: A pilotless aircraft.

emergency: An unexpected situation that calls for immediate action.

investigation: To study by closely examining.

remote: Far away.

signal: A radio wave that transmits a message or warning.

volunteer: Someone who does something to help because they want to do it.

FOR MORE INFORMATION

BOOKS

Idzikowski, Lisa. *Search-and-Rescue Animals.* New York, NY: Enslow Publishing, 2019.

Nagle, Frances. *Coast Guard Boats to the Rescue!* New York, NY: Gareth Stevens Publishing, 2023.

Newcomb, Tim. *Search and Rescue Team.* Broomall, PA: Mason Crest, 2016.

WEBSITES

Civil Air Patrol U.S. Air Force Auxiliary - Youth
www.gocivilairpatrol.com/join/youth-in-cadet-program
Learn about the Civil Air Patrol's Cadet Program for youth between ages 12 to 18.

Coast Guard Missions
www.gocoastguard.com/about/missions
Read about the U.S. Coast Guard and learn about its search and rescue operations.

Search and Rescue
www.sarsat.noaa.gov/search-and-rescue/
Learn about different types of search and rescue operations on the National Oceanic and Atmospheric Administration (NOAA)'s website.

INDEX